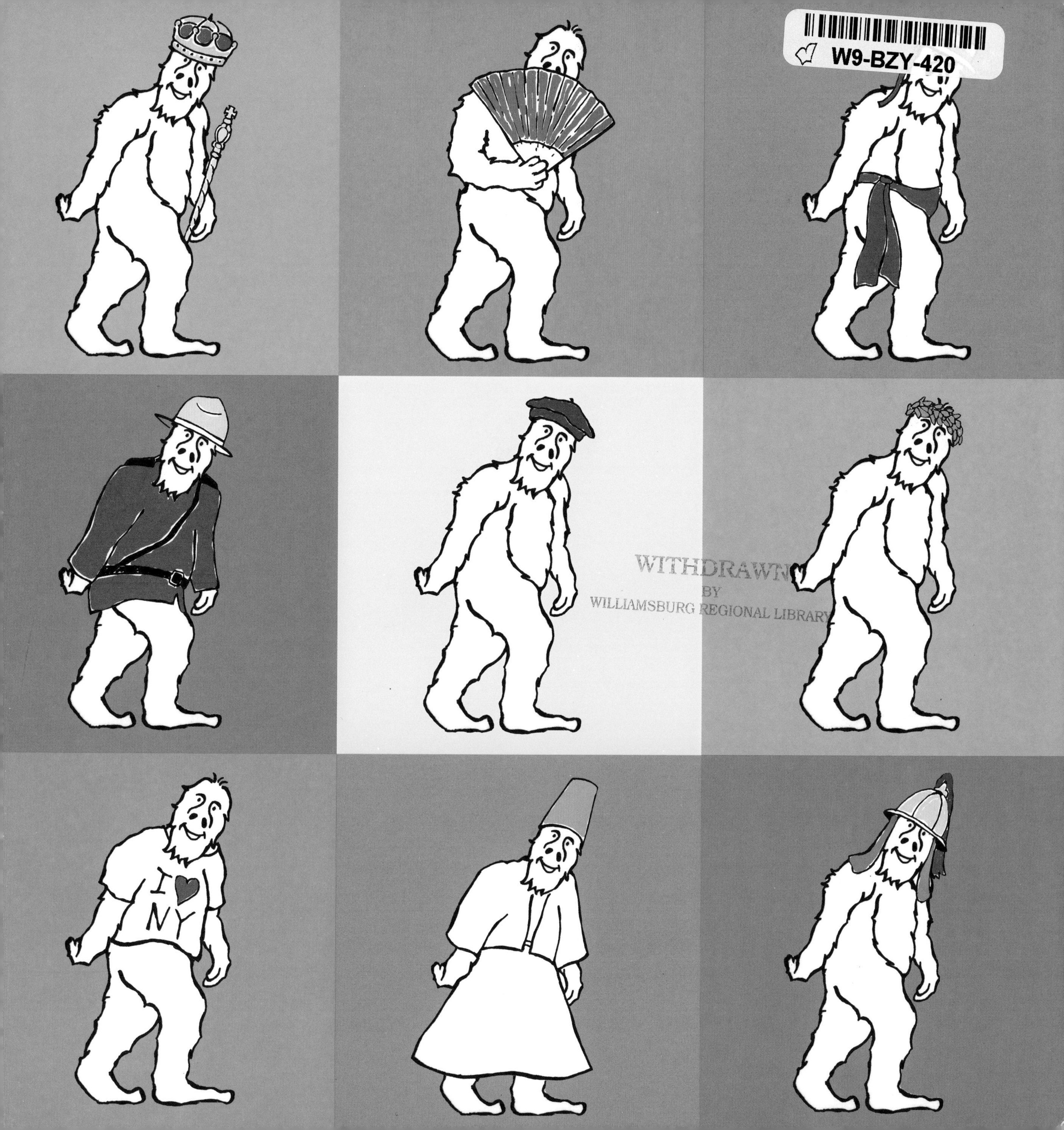

I ♥ NY

A SPECTACULAR SEEK AND FIND CHALLENGE FOR ALL AGES!
BIGFOOT™
Visits the Big Cities of the World

D. L. MILLER

HAPPY FOX
BOOKS

For Mom and Dad, and the Miller brothers who grew up in our little house nestled in the mountains of Western Maryland, where we spent many a day exploring the beauty and mysteries of the woods and creek bottoms just outside our front door.

—D. L. Miller

A Big Thank You

to all the BigFoot hunters around the world who not only believe that our big furry friend really does exist, but more importantly that he continues to inspire us to go outside and explore this great big world.

A Special Thank You

to the wonderful folks at Fox Chapel Publishing for bringing the BigFoot Seek and Find series to life, especially…

Publisher: Alan Giagnocavo
Vice President – Content: Christopher Reggio
Senior Editor: Laura Taylor
Managing Editor: Melissa Younger
Contributing Editor: Jeremy Hauck
Graphic Design: Kate Lanphier

BigFoot Visits the Big Cities of the World is an original work, first published in 2018 by Fox Chapel Publishing Company, Inc.

ISBN 978-1-64124-001-7

The Cataloging-in-Publication Data is on file with the Library of Congress.

To learn more about the other great books from Fox Chapel Publishing, or to find a retailer near you, call toll-free 800-457-9112 or visit us at *www.FoxChapelPublishing.com.*

We are always looking for talented authors. To submit an idea, please send a brief inquiry to acquisitions@foxchapelpublishing.com.

Printed in China
First printing

Shutterstock photos: 3000ad (39 middle right); 4kclips (35 middle); Alp Aksoy (42 bottom); Babich Alexander (15 middle left); Bobo Ling (27 middle); Brent Hofacker (30 bottom); Brian Minkoff (19 bottom); Bufflerump (11 bottom left); cge2010 (22 bottom); Chung Chih (39 bottom right); Dan Schreiber (34 middle right); DayOwl (30 middle); DemarK (38 bottom); Denizce (42 middle); dibrova (35 bottom); Everett Historical (11 top, 23 middle); Executioner (26 bottom); Faraways (43 bottom); hurricanehank (15 bottom); Hurst Photo (39 middle left); Janet Faye Hastings (34 middle left); Jiri Hera (7 middle right); JuliaLerma (23 bottom); Juri Pozzi (27 bottom); Keeton Gale (31 center); lazyllama (15 middle right); lynx_v (14 top); Maks Ershov (35 top); Marco Rubino (10 bottom); Mehmet Cetin (43 top); MrPhotoMania (42 top); Nadiia_foto (7 top); Nancy Ann Ellis (10 middle); Nataliya Nazarova (23 top); NathalieB (15 top); naytoong (39 bottom left); Nickolay Stanev (34 top); Nicku (7 bottom); NIPAPORN PANYACHAROEN (26 middle); Olga Utchenko (31 bottom); pavalena (22 top); Peter Nadolski (18 middle); petereleven (19 middle right); pisaphotography (10 top); Production Perig (7 middle left); ptaa2010 (39 middle center); Rainer Lesniewski (11 bottom right); Rob van Esch (43 middle); Roberto Machado Rodriguez (30 top); Rudy Riva (5 top right); S.Borisov (14 bottom); S-F (6 bottom, 18 bottom left); Sean Pavone (26 top); seeshooteatrepeat (19 middle left); Serghei Starus (14 middle); Sergii Rudiuk (38 top); ShenTao (34 bottom); Stephen Mcsweeny (18 bottom right); TTstudio (6 top); Vera Petruk (5 bottom); William Perugini (31 top); Yarygin (43 bottom inset); Zanna Holstova (27 top); Zhao jian kang (39 top)

Photos on pages 18 (top right) and 19 (top right) by Kate Lanphier.

BIGFOOT CONTENTS

Grab your passport and plane tickets: it's time to follow BigFoot into the world's most interesting urban vistas . . . and maybe get a little lost in the crowds yourself!

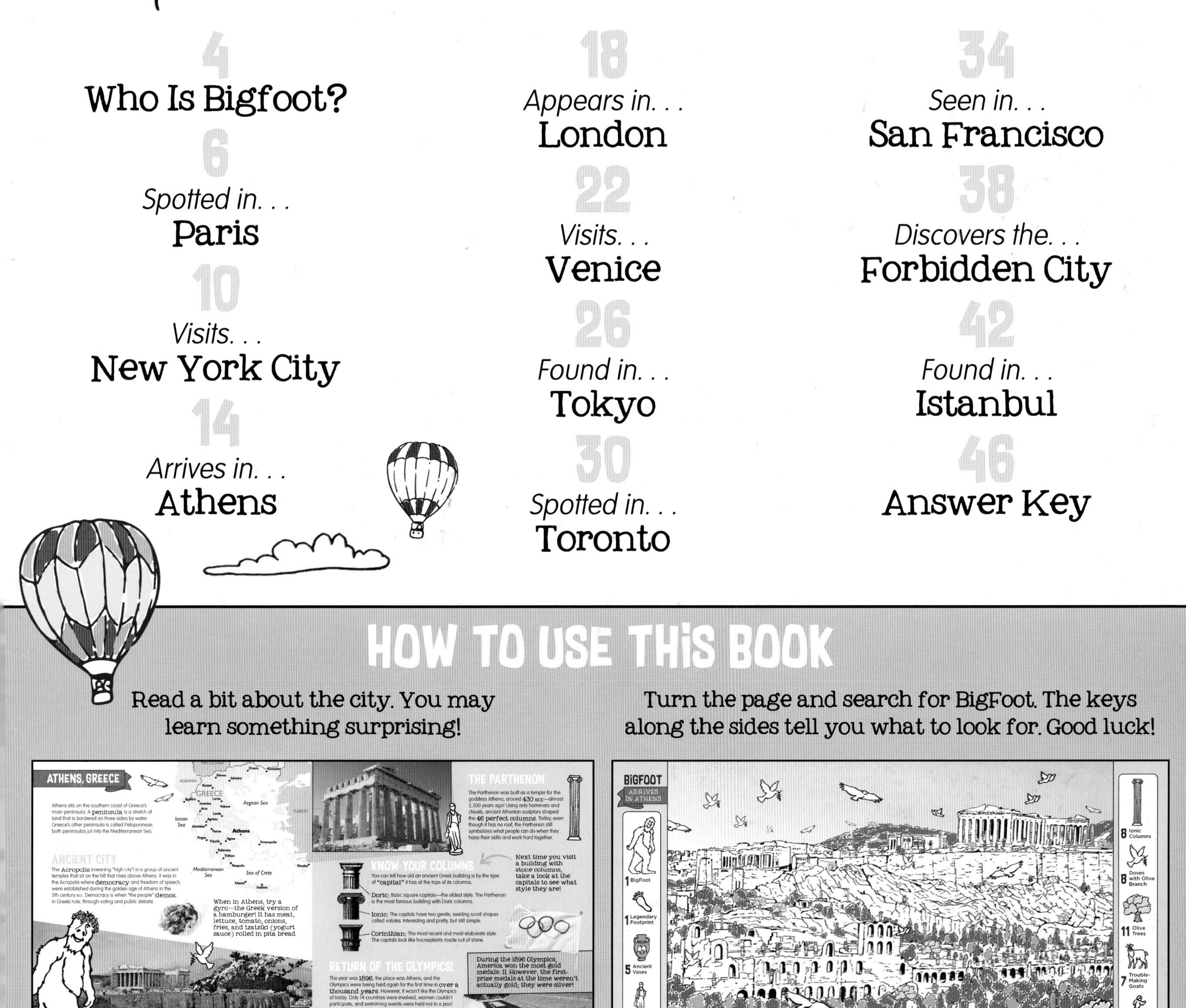

HOW TO USE THIS BOOK

Read a bit about the city. You may learn something surprising!

Turn the page and search for BigFoot. The keys along the sides tell you what to look for. Good luck!

WHO iS BiGFOOT?

Stories about the infamous BigFoot have been handed down from generation to generation in many countries around the world. Although his history is a bit **unknown**, many theories have been explored over the years to explain why people continue to see this mysterious creature no matter where they live. Some believe he's a **giant bear** that has been seen walking around on two legs, while others believe he may be a **giant gorilla** roaming the forests.

HAVE YOU SEEN A REAL BiGFOOT?

Although descriptions of the giant, fury creature differ from region to region, they all share several common details: a large, fury human-like creature standing **7 feet (2.3 m) to 9 feet (3 m) tall.** Reports suggest that BigFoot is brown, although many have also reported seeing black, gray, white, and greenish-blue BigFoots. Some descriptions also include details such as **large eyes** with a very pronounced brow, and a large forehead. The top of his head is often described as rounded with a narrow top, similar to the shape of a large gorilla. If you see someone walking around that looks like this, you're probably looking at BigFoot!

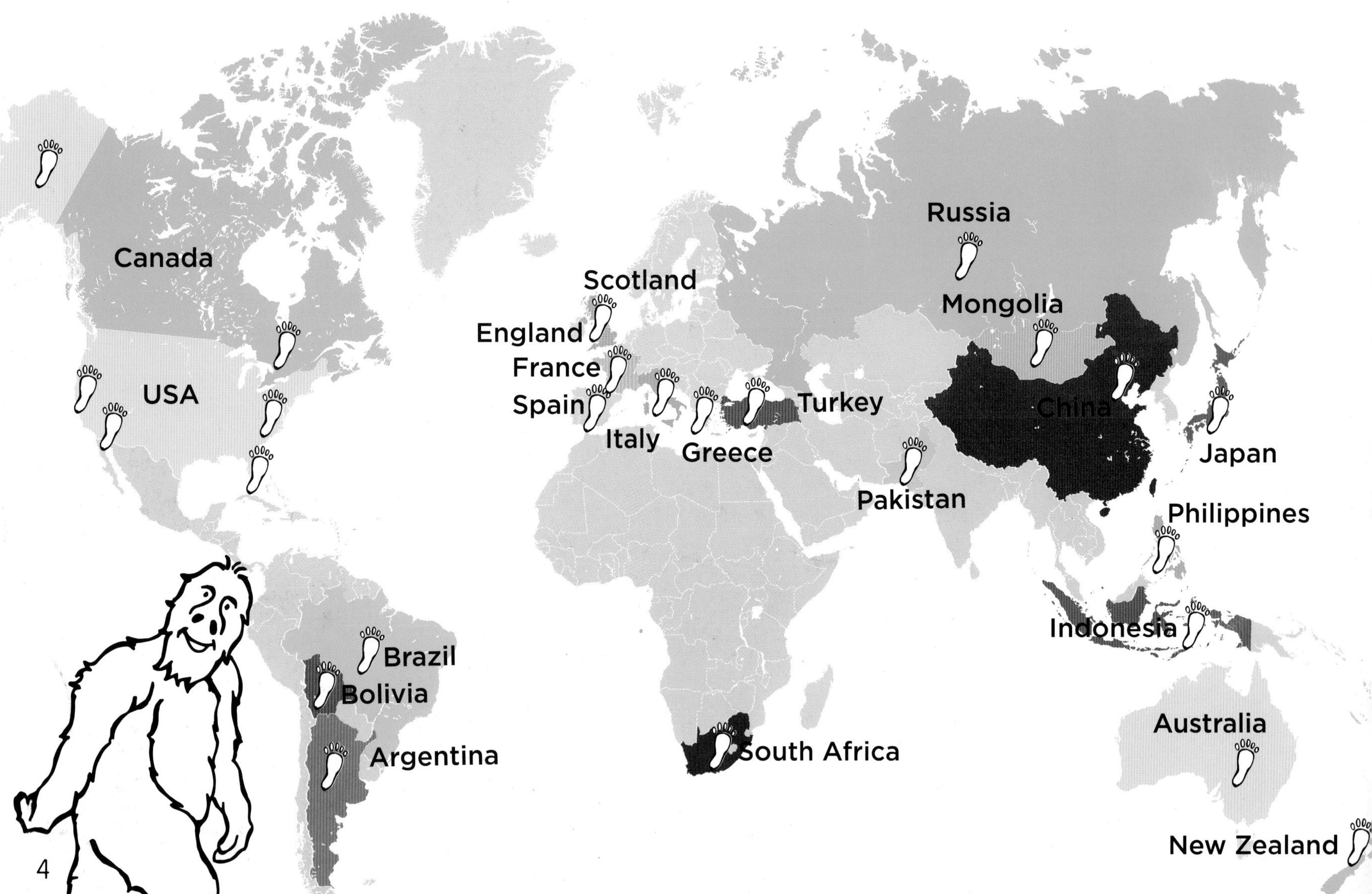

WHERE DID THE NAME *BIGFOOT* COME FROM?

In the 1800s, the name **BigFoot** was first used in America to describe huge **grizzly bears** that were spotted in parts of the United States. Some believe that **David Thompson**, a man crossing the Rocky Mountains in the winter of 1811, discovered the first real set of BigFoot footprints in the snow. The tracks were too big for even the largest known bear. The name was again used when people started spotting massive, **human-like** footprints on the forest floor that kind of resembled a large bear's. These footprints were about 24 inches (61 cm) long and 8 inches (20 cm) wide, more than **double** the size of an average adult shoe. Many people believe that these big footprints are enough proof that our BigFoot really does exist!

BIG FOOT XING

DUE TO SIGHTINGS IN THE AREA OF A CREATURE RESEMBLING "BIG FOOT" THIS SIGN HAS BEEN POSTED FOR YOUR SAFETY

Frame 352 of the Patterson-Gimlin film, taken in the fall of 1967 in Northern California's **Six Rivers National Forest** by Roger Patterson and Bob Gimlin. While some people believe the **BigFoot** shown here was only a person in a costume, others believe it's the real deal.

It's been reported by some that BigFoot can run up to 30 miles per hour (48 kph)—the average human runs half that speed!

BIGFOOT GOES BY MANY NAMES

BigFoot is known by many different names around the world, including the most common: **Sasquatch**. So don't forget to tell people you're going **"Squatching"** next time you decide to search for our giant, furry friend. What do other parts of the world call BigFoot?

- **Barmanou** (Pakistan)
- **Basajuan** (Spain)
- **Big Greyman** (Scotland)
- **Gin-Sung** (China)
- **Hibagon** (Japan)
- **Kapre** (Philippines)
- **Kushtaka** (Alaska, USA)
- **Mapinguari** (Brazil and Bolivia)
- **Menk** (Russia)
- **Moehau** (New Zealand)
- **Mogollon Monster** (Arizona, USA)
- **Orange Pendek** (Indonesia)
- **Skunk Ape** (Florida, USA)
- **Ucu** (Argentina)
- **Waterbobbejaan** (South Africa)
- **Wendigo** (Canada)
- **Woodwosa** (England)
- **Yeren** (Mongolia)
- **Yeti** (Russia)
- **Yowie** (Australia)

NOTRE DAME CATHEDRAL

It took nearly **200 years** to build the large church called Notre Dame (pronounced "no-tra dahm")—from 1163 to 1345 during the Middle Ages. It has beautiful stained glass windows, majestic organs, and several bells, the largest weighing **13 tons**. Get your exercise by climbing 387 steps to the top of one of the cathedral's towers! On the outside of the building are lots of **gargoyles**—stone statues of creepy creatures—that had two functions: they were supposed to scare away evil spirits and they served as rain gutters to carry water off the roof and away from the building. The cathedral is the landmark used in Victor Hugo's famous book ***The Hunchback of Notre Dame***. . . and in a famous animated movie!

Every seven years the Eiffel Tower gets a fresh coat of brown paint.

WORK OF ART? OR FACTORY CHiMNEY?

How many skyscrapers can you count in the seek-and-find picture? One . . . OK, just one. Aside from church bell towers, Europeans usually don't have tall buildings in their historical city centers. They want their cathedrals and palaces to be the focus. But sometimes exceptions are made . . .

Built by **Gustave Eiffel** in 1889 for the World's Fair, the Eiffel Tower is made of iron, measures **1,063 feet tall** (twice as tall as the Statue of Liberty!), and weighs 11,100 tons. There are 20,000 light bulbs that make the tower sparkle each night. You can ride in an elevator to the top and see Paris like a bird would!

Though Parisians today love their *tour Eiffel* (pronounced "tur ee-FELL"), back when it was being built some people said it looked like a **"gigantic black factory chimney."** Lucky for BigFoot, most people disagreed!

THE LOUVRE

World's largest **art museum**. The Louvre (rhymes with "move") started out as a fortress in the 12th century and then became the home for French kings in 1546. Soon after the **French Revolution**, on August 10, 1793, the building became a museum open to the public. An average of 15,000 people visit the Louvre each day to see famous works like Leonardo da Vinci's ***Mona Lisa***.

THE "CITY OF LIGHT"

In the late 1600s, to solve a problem with street crime and make their city safer, Parisians had to hang **lanterns** in their windows at night. And so Paris first acquired its nickname, the "City of Light." This nickname also comes from so many writers and artists **(Picasso! Hemingway!)** who have lived in Paris — their paintings and stories are like lights showing us new ideas.

YUM!

Those long, skinny loaves of bread are called baguettes ("bag-ets")—320 of them are eaten per second in France!

UP, UP, AND AWAY

On **November 21, 1783**, Jean-François Pilâtre de Rozier and the Marquis d'Arlandes lifted off in a hot-air balloon made out of cloth. They kept the hot air coming by adding straw to a fire in a special stove under the balloon. It was like a campfire in the sky! For **25 minutes** they floated over Paris. By the time they landed about 5 miles away, they had made history: mankind's first untethered flight.

Among the people on the ground watching that day, one couldn't help but be impressed by the flying balloon: **Benjamin Franklin**.

BiGFOOT
SPOTTED IN PARIS
1 BigFoot
1 Legendary Footprint
8 Flying Biplanes
4 Inspired Artists

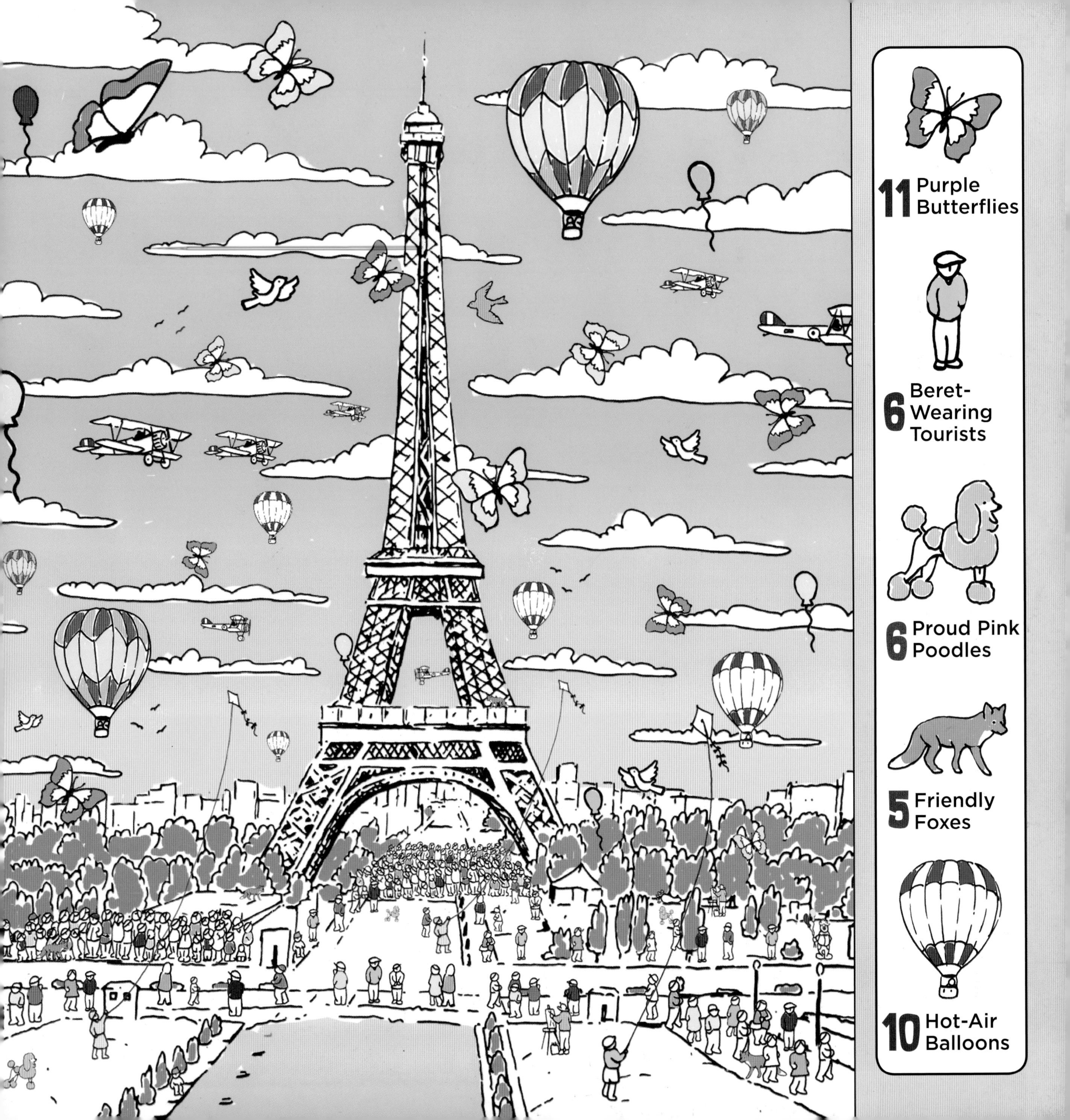
11 Purple Butterflies
6 Beret-Wearing Tourists
6 Proud Pink Poodles
5 Friendly Foxes
10 Hot-Air Balloons

HUMBLE ROOTS

Times Square used to be a dirt road intersection called **Longacre Square**. After the ***New York Times*** newspaper built its offices there in 1904, Mayor George McClellan renamed the intersection **"Times Square."** Though the newspaper offices have moved, you can still see the original building at 1 Times Square!

The first Times Square **New Year's Eve ball drop** came down on December 31, 1907. The ball drop has become a huge event that millions of Americans watch every year on TV.

Many different languages can be heard on the streets of New York City: 51% of New Yorkers speak more than one language. *Ciao!*

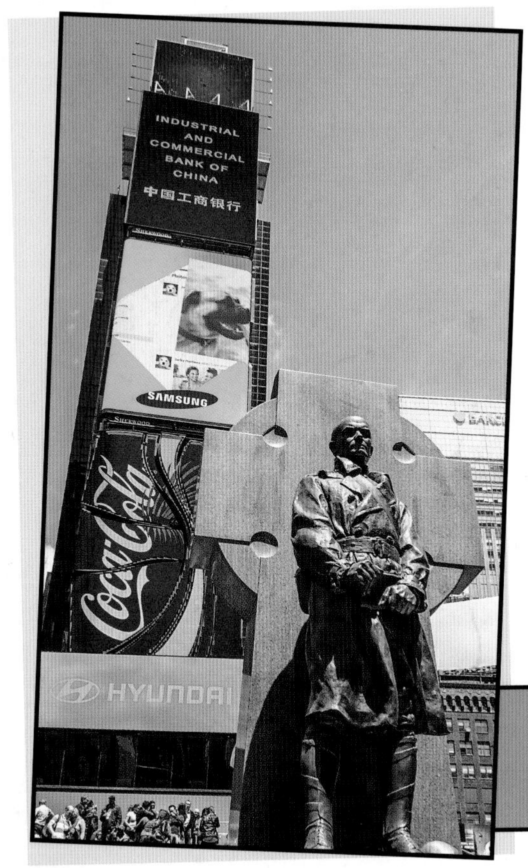

THAT iS SPECTACULAR!

Don't call them "billboards"! On Times Square, the huge signs go by the name **"spectaculars."** They started out as regular billboards but got bigger and brighter over the years. These days, they have millions of tiny **LED lights** and gigantic screens that play video ads—how spectacular is that?

The **Coca-Cola** sign hanging in Times Square has been in the same spot since the 1930s!

GRAFFITI CLEANUP

Back in the 1970s and 1980s, New York City subways were covered in graffiti. But then the city went on a major cleaning spree, and on **May 12, 1989**, announced that New York was a clean-train city!

The first rides on New York City's subway were taken on **October 27, 1904**.

EXTRA! EXTRA!

In the 19th century, boys called **"newsies"** collected **newspapers** early in the morning from the printer and sold them on the streets of the city. In **1899**, they went on strike for better pay and working conditions. Led by boys with nicknames like Kid Blink and Racetrack Higgens, they were viewed as heroes by many, and inspired the Disney musical *Newsies*!

The city is made up of 5 boroughs (sections): Manhattan, Brooklyn, The Bronx, Queens, and Staten Island.

TAXI!

In a city where most people don't own cars, the yellow cab is king. New York has more than **13,000** of them!

BIGFOOT
VISITS NEW YORK
1 BigFoot
1 Legendary Footprint
5 Crazy Coyotes
5 Pink Shirt Ladies
HOTEL
HERSHEY'S
MILK CHOCOLATE
SAMSUNG
YAHOO!
TOMMY
TOMMY
NYC

NYC
TIMES
SQUAR
MAMA MI
PHANTOM
WEST
SIDE
STORY
JVC
sbarro
sbarro
sbarro
sbarro
sbarro
Fashion
3 Green Balloons
7 Camera-Toting Tourists
4 Police Officers
14 Feeding Pigeons
3 Balloon Sellers

ATHENS, GREECE

Athens sits on the southern coast of Greece's main peninsula. A **peninsula** is a stretch of land that is bordered on three sides by water. Greece's other peninsula is called Peloponnese; both peninsulas jut into the Mediterranean Sea.

ANCIENT CITY

The **Acropolis** (meaning "high city") is a group of ancient temples that sit on the hill that rises above Athens. It was in the Acropolis where **democracy** and freedom of speech were established during the golden age of Athens in the 5th century BCE. Democracy is when "the people" (**demos**, in Greek) rule, through voting and public debate.

When in Athens, try a gyro—the Greek version of a hamburger! It has meat, lettuce, tomato, onions, fries, and tzatziki (yogurt sauce) rolled in pita bread.

THE PARTHENON

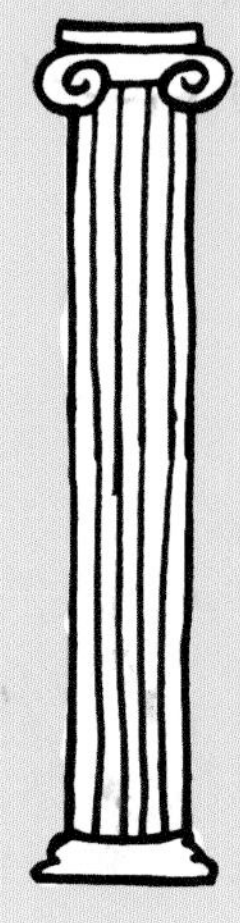

The Parthenon was built as a temple for the goddess Athena, around **430** BCE—almost 2,500 years ago! Using only hammers and chisels, ancient Athenian sculptors shaped the **46 perfect columns**. Today, even though it has no roof, the Parthenon still symbolizes what people can do when they hone their skills and work hard together.

KNOW YOUR COLUMNS

You can tell how old an ancient Greek building is by the type of **"capital"** it has at the tops of its columns.

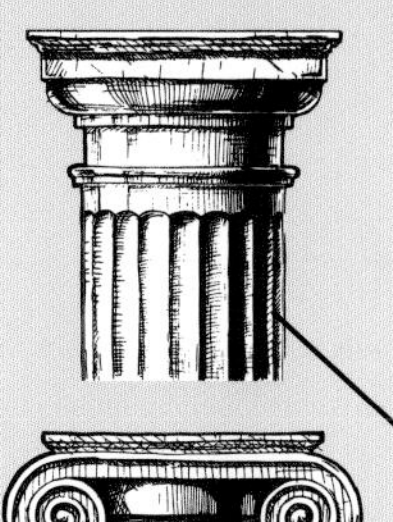

Doric: Basic square capitals—the oldest style. The Parthenon is the most famous building with Doric columns.

Ionic: The capitals have two gentle, swirling scroll shapes called *volutes*. Interesting and pretty, but still simple.

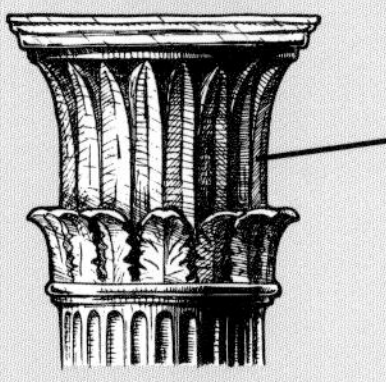

Corinthian: The most recent and most elaborate style. The capitals look like houseplants made out of stone.

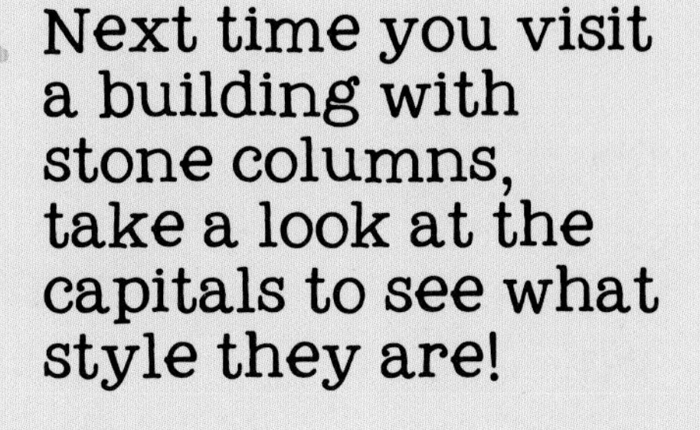

Next time you visit a building with stone columns, take a look at the capitals to see what style they are!

RETURN OF THE OLYMPICS!

The year was **1896**, the place was Athens, and the Olympics were being held again for the first time in **over a thousand years**. However, it wasn't like the Olympics of today. Only 14 countries were involved, women couldn't participate, and swimming events were held not in a pool but in a choppy ocean inlet. Nevertheless, the first modern Olympics were a huge success! **Every four years** since (except during World Wars I and II), they have been held, a celebration of peaceful competition among nations.

During the 1896 Olympics, America won the most gold medals: 11. However, the first-prize medals at the time weren't actually gold; they were silver!

BIGFOOT
ARRIVES IN ATHENS
1 BigFoot
1 Legendary Footprint
5 Ancient Vases
3 Greek Statues

8 Ionic Columns
8 Doves with Olive Branch
11 Olive Trees
7 Trouble-Making Goats
5 Olympic Runners

WHO IS BIG BEN?

Though everyone calls the 315-foot (96 m)-tall clock tower at the Houses of Parliament "Big Ben," the clock tower's name is actually the **Elizabeth Tower**; Big Ben is the name of the **15-ton bell** hanging in the belfry of the tower. It chimed for the first time on July 11, 1859. Each of the tower's 4 huge clock faces is 23 feet (7 m) across and made of hundreds of sections of white frosted glass. Each hour hand is over 9 feet (3 m) long, and the minute hands are each 14 feet (4 m) long; naturally, the clock keeps perfect time.

The clock at the top of Elizabeth Tower keeps accurate time—most of the time! On New Year's Eve 1962, heavy snow and ice slowed the clock's hands, and Big Ben chimed in the New Year **10 minutes late**.

ROUTEMASTER RED

London's famous red **double-decker buses**, called "Routemasters," first appeared in 1954. On some models the top level has no roof, so it's like riding in a convertible bus! These buses used to have a conductor who stood on an open platform where passengers could quickly hop on or off. Although the buses no longer have conductors and open platforms, one "heritage" Routemaster is still used, especially by tourists wanting an old-fashioned London experience!

Fish and chips (fries) is the most popular English take-out meal. It became popular during World War II when fish was plentiful and other foods weren't.

DRIVING LEFT, STEERING RIGHT

In England, cars drive in the left lane and the steering wheel is on the right side of the car. That may seem odd, but it makes some sense. Way back when people traveled by horse, the roads weren't always safe and sometimes fights broke out. People stayed on the left side of the road so their swords (carried on their right hip) could be easily grabbed and used to meet an oncoming attacker. **The General Highways Act of 1773** made this left-lane system official in England.

BRITISH ENGLISH VS. AMERICAN ENGLISH

It wasn't so long ago that English people and Americans sounded pretty much the same when they talked. As late as the 1700s, both spoke **"rhotic"** English, which means they pronounced their Rs (as in "card"). But after American independence, **upper-class** Londoners started dropping their Rs when they spoke (so "card" sounded like "cahd"), to separate themselves more from the lower classes.

In the **1920s**, the **BBC** (British Broadcasting Corporation) required its announcers to use this upper-class accent, officially called "Received Pronunciation," in radio broadcasts, and it became the sound of how the rest of the world thought all English people spoke.

Many Londoners enjoy afternoon tea as a way to fight the midday munchies. Tea is served along with scones, cookies, cakes, and small sandwiches.

RIDING THE TUBE

If someone in London asks you where the **"tube"** is, they're not searching for toothpaste! They're looking for London's famous **underground subway**, officially called the **London Underground**. It opened in 1863, which makes it the oldest subway system in the world. With 11 lines and 270 stations throughout London and surrounding counties, tube rides can put any visitor in a London state of mind!

BIGFOOT
APPEARS IN LONDON
1 BigFoot
1 Legendary Footprint
7 Red Phone Boxes
12 Cawing Ravens

9 Happy Chimney Sweeps
9 Restless Raven Keepers
4 Gold Crowns
1 Royal Queen
7 Red Umbrella Walkers

VENiCE, ITALY

The city of Venice is actually a **cluster of islands** in northeastern Italy. There's hardly any solid ground in this city—it's all mud, stones, and sand, washed there by the River Po. All of the city's grand palaces and churches, and all the little sidewalk shops and cafes, stand on foundations of **tree trunks**—millions of them—stuck in the mud. Some of the buildings settle a little bit deeper into the mud every year; no wonder people call Venice the **"Sinking City."**

SLOVENIA
VENICE
CROATIA
FRANCE
Bosnia & Herzegovina
Ligurian Sea
ITALY
ROME
Adriatic Sea
Mediterranean Sea
Ionian Sea

There are about 400 gondolas in Venice. How many can you count in the seek-and-find picture?

NO CAR, NO PROBLEM

Unlike most cities in the world, Venice is a city without buses, cars, buses, subways, or wide streets. Instead, people take boats that glide along canals crisscrossing the city like streets. These **canals** are filled with boats of all kinds: mail boats, police boats, water taxis, and of course, **gondolas**.

CiTY OF GONDOLAS

Only **two people** fit comfortably in a gondola at one time, which may be why they've earned a reputation as a romantic form of transport. Using only **one oar**, a *gondolier* rows his gondola very slowly, about as fast as someone walking, along the blue-green canals, sometimes singing beautiful songs in Italian. The **gondolier** stands up because he always has to be able to see sandbars where his gondola might get stuck. To help steer in narrow canals, he will sometimes use his foot to push off a nearby building.

HiGH WATER MARK

Every winter the **Adriatic Sea** floods into Venice so often that the Venetians have a name for it: the *acqua alta*, or **"high water."** Briny, fishy water covers the sidewalks, fills the plazas, and seeps around front doors. Not to worry, though: Venetians always have a pair of high rubber boots at the ready!

Lots of cats slink around St. Mark's Plaza and other sites in Venice. In the late 20th century, a gray tabby named Neno loved exploring the city and riding on boats.

MARCO! POLO!

Maybe the most famous Venetian in history, **Marco Polo (1254–1324)** had the extremely rare experience of living in Asia as a European traveller during the Middle Ages. He spent 17 years in China before returning to Venice in 1295. Marco Polo saw **paper money** being used in China and brought the idea home. Until then, paper money had not yet replaced precious metals.

CARNiVAL

Every **February**, Venetians dress up in kind-of funny, kind-of scary costumes to celebrate Carnival. Carnival is a time of feasts and parades before the traditional fasting season of **Lent**. Tourists are encouraged to buy masks and join in the fun!

BiGFOOT
VISITS
VENICE
1 BigFoot
1 Legendary Footprint
7 Orange Tabbies
8 Red Canopy Gondolas

6 Pink Joyful Jesters
6 Resting White Felines
5 Winged Lions
8 Trios of Wandering Minstrels
8 Boatless Gondoliers

TOYKO, JAPAN

ONCE EDO, NOW TOKYO

Tokyo was founded in the **1100s** as a little fishing village but it had a different name—**Edo**. By the 1700s, it is thought to have been the biggest city in the world. When the Japanese emperor moved to Edo in 1868 and the people there began to modernize, adopting Western-style clothing and business practices, the city became known as Tokyo, **"eastern capital."**

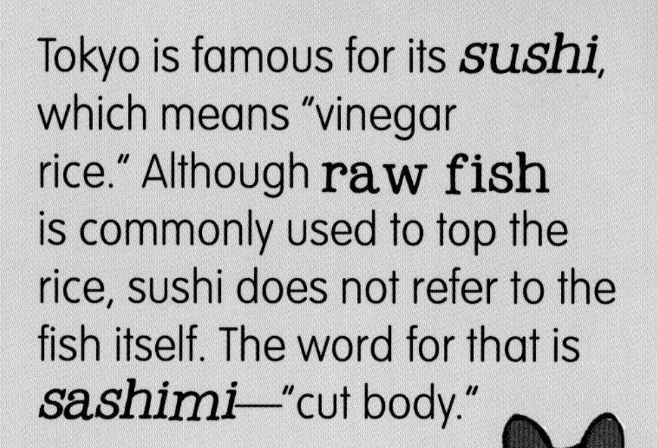

Tokyo is famous for its ***sushi***, which means "vinegar rice." Although **raw fish** is commonly used to top the rice, sushi does not refer to the fish itself. The word for that is ***sashimi***—"cut body."

***Shinkansen*, or bullet trains, zip people up and down Japan going well over 100 miles per hour (161 kph)!**

HOW *PAKU* BECAME PAC-MAN

One day in the late 1970s, a young video game programmer named **Toru Iwatani** went to a Tokyo **pizza shop**. His job at the time was to make a video game that looked fun for both boys and girls to play. Eyeing the pizza he had bought, with one slice removed, gave him an idea: a friendly yellow circle we know as Pac-Man (*paku* means **"chomp"** in Japanese) who gobbles up pieces of cake and little dots while running from ghosts.

Over 1/3 of Tokyo is covered with forests—plenty of space for BigFoot to hide from crowds!

LAND OF FANTASTIC CREATURES

Mythical Japanese **dragons** don't have wings or breathe fire. Instead, they have long, slithering bodies and swim in the sea. The Japanese dragon, or ***ryū***, symbolizes weather and good fortune rather than trouble and hoarded treasure like the European dragon.

PAPER CRANES

Japanese legend has it that if you make **1,000** origami (folded paper) cranes, you get to make **one wish** that will come true. Frequently given in Japan as wedding or baby shower gifts, origami cranes hung in your house are supposed to bring you the best of luck.

GEISHAS

Faces painted white, hair pinned up in traditional style, and beautiful silk kimonos flowing, geishas walk to their next teahouse appointment where they will entertain powerful businessmen or government officials. *Geisha* means **"art-person"** or **"skill-person,"** and since the 1600s, young women have trained for years to become geishas. Geishas can perform complicated traditional Japanese dances, have witty conversations, and even play the ***shamisen***, a stringed instrument like the banjo.

Tanuki are very real animals. They look like a mix between raccoons and foxes: cuddly, furry animals that, like raccoons, **come out at night** and eat just about anything. In folktales, tanuki trick people by taking on different shapes—a wise monk, for instance, or even a teapot!

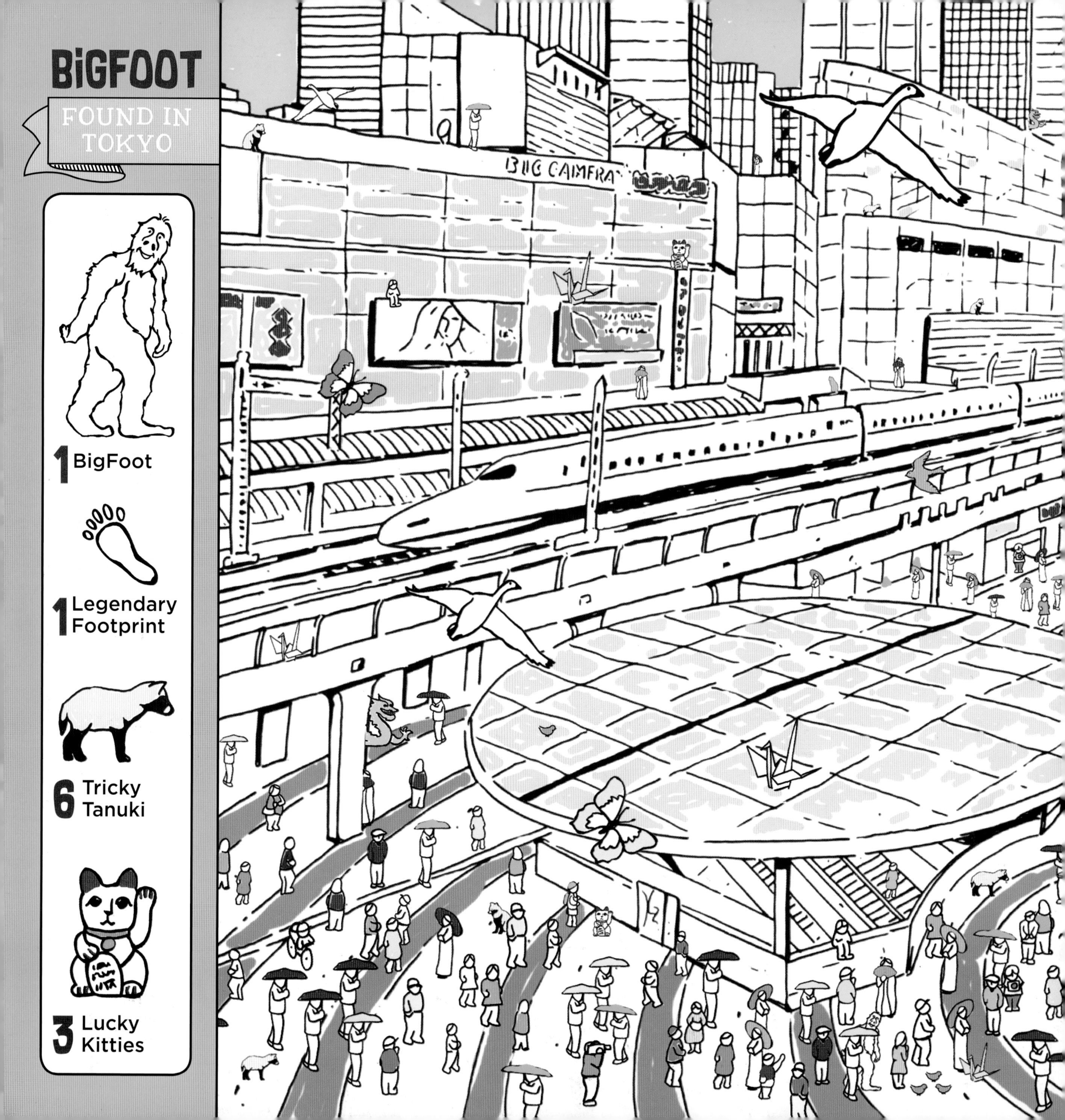
BIGFOOT
FOUND IN TOKYO
1 BigFoot
1 Legendary Footprint
6 Tricky Tanuki
3 Lucky Kitties
BIG CAMERA

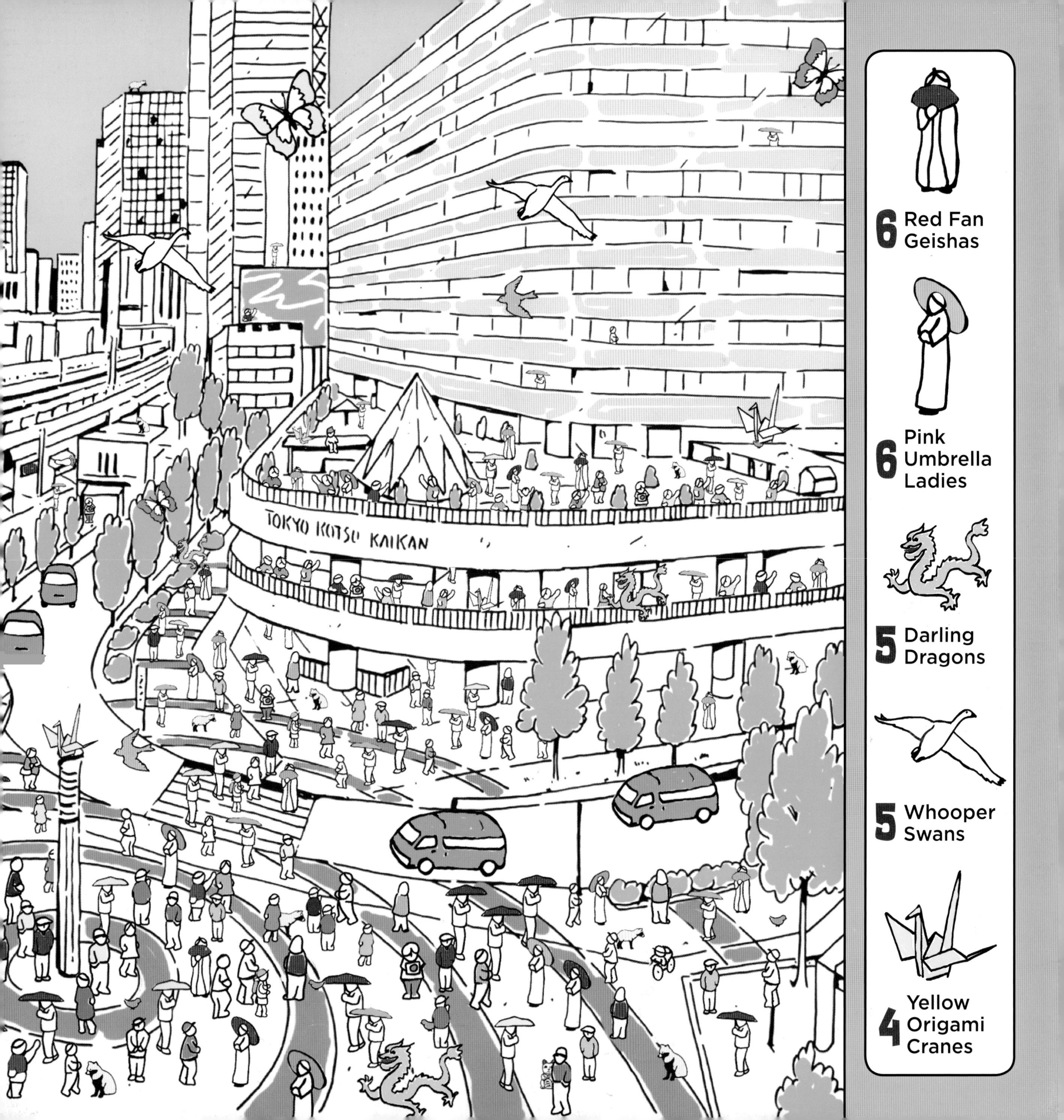
TOKYO KOTSU KAIKAN
6 Red Fan Geishas
6 Pink Umbrella Ladies
5 Darling Dragons
5 Whooper Swans
4 Yellow Origami Cranes

TORONTO, CANADA

ULTIMATE SKYSCRAPER

The most famous building in Canada is the **CN Tower.** When it was built in the 1970s, it was the world's tallest freestanding structure. Not anymore, though: it's number 8! "CN" stands for **Canadian National**, the name of the government-owned railroad company that originally built the tower. Although the tower's main job is to help Toronto stand out among world cities and offer breathtaking views to tourists, its original purpose was to **broadcast TV and radio signals**, a job it still performs today for more than 30 stations.

At **1,122** feet (342 m) up, there is a room with thick glass panels in the floor so you can sit and look down at the ground—if you're not too scared of heights! Or you could go higher and try the **EdgeWalk**. Harnessed to a ring on the tower's roof, you inch along a narrow ledge—with no railing—1,168 feet (356 m) up!

The World Poutine Eating Contest is held every year on Toronto's Yonge-Dundas Square. *Poutine ("poo-TEEN")*, a French slang word for "mess," is a heavy dish made from French fries and cheese curds with gravy.

WORLD CITY

Studies have found that Toronto, Canada's largest city, is one of the most **diverse cities** in the world. Half its population was born abroad, in over **200 foreign countries**! And more than 140 different languages are spoken in Toronto, with **Farsi** (Iran) and **Tagalog** (Philippines) among those on the rise. Neighborhoods like Little Italy, Portugal Village, and Greektown all have their own cultural festivals to brighten the calendar.

Toronto has always been seen as a good place to move to. After the **American Revolution**, people in the States who wanted to stay loyal to England moved to Toronto in droves, and to this day Toronto has a welcoming vibe.

The word *Toronto* comes from the Mohawk word *Tkaranto*: "where there are trees standing in the water."

BIRDER'S PARADISE

Toronto is well known for its abundance of winged neighbors. **More than 300** native kinds of birds have been spotted in the city's parks—no wonder the baseball team's name is the **Blue Jays!** The best time to go bird-watching in Toronto is **mid-May**, when flocks of birds, including tiny hummingbirds and honking geese, return from their winter migrations in the south.

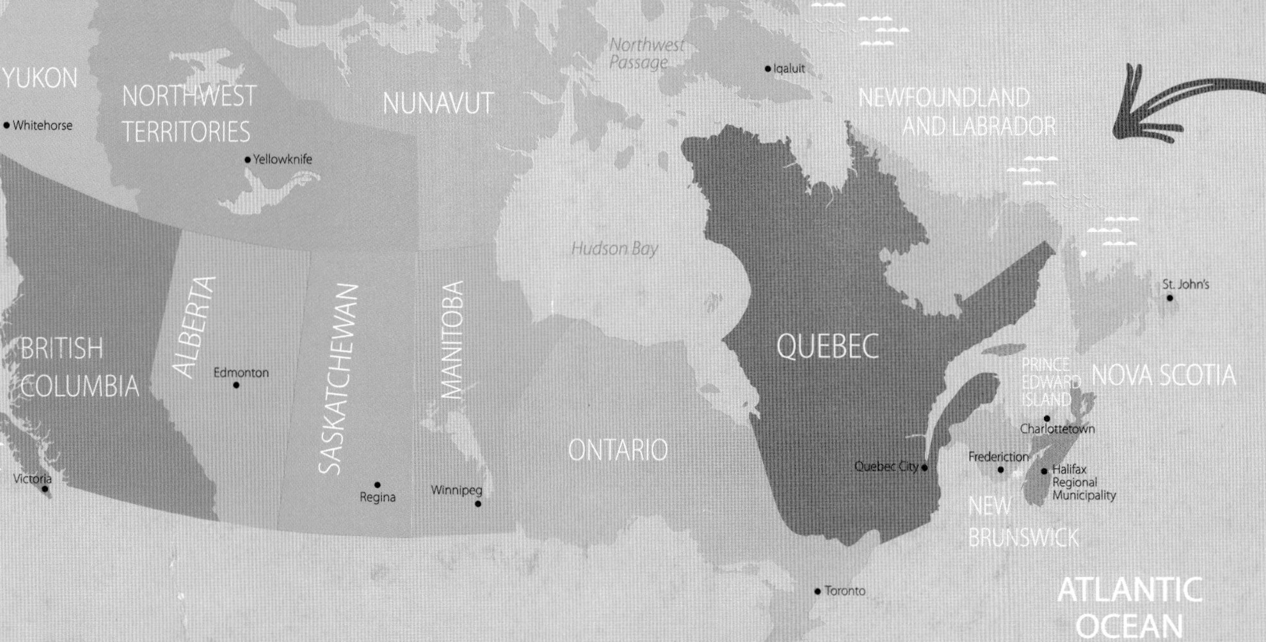

Instead of states, Canada has **ten provinces** and **three territories**. Toronto is located in the province of **Ontario**, the most populated in the country and the one going the farthest south, sharing the Great Lakes with the United States.

BiGFOOT
SPOTTED IN TORONTO
1 BigFoot
1 Legendary Footprint
12 Honking Geese
10 Canadian Flag Sailboats

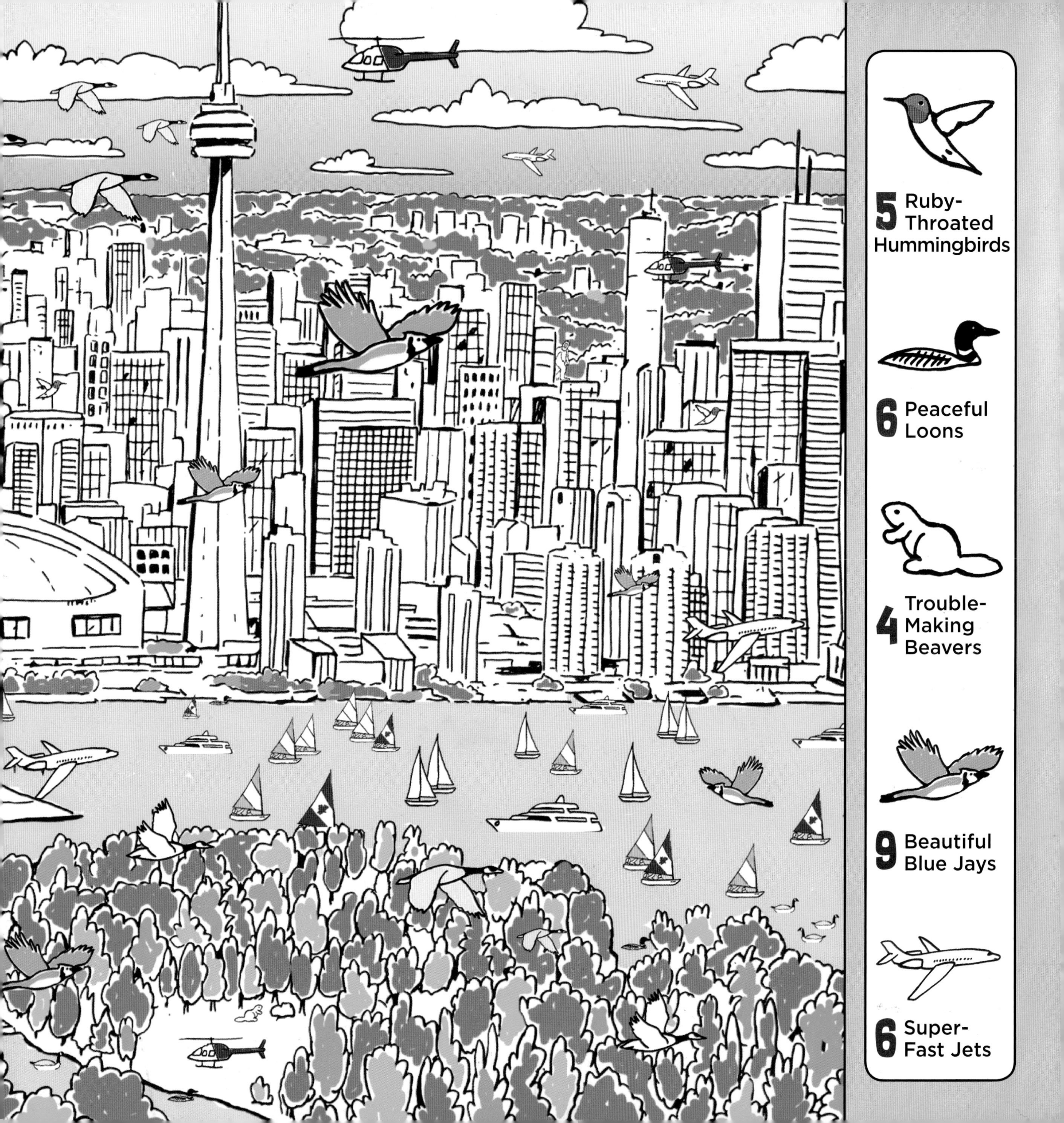
5 Ruby-Throated Hummingbirds
6 Peaceful Loons
4 Trouble-Making Beavers
9 Beautiful Blue Jays
6 Super-Fast Jets

SAN FRANCiSCO, USA

San Francisco, California, is the largest city in what people call the **Bay Area**. The Bay Area includes the cities of Oakland, Berkeley, and San Jose, all of which surround the huge San Francisco Bay on the Pacific Ocean. The Bay Area is home to more than **7 million people**.

San Francisco takes its name from a Spanish mission named after **Saint Francis of Assisi** (1181–1226). The mission, an outpost of the Roman Catholic Church, was founded in **1776** to convert local people. Though the mission fell into disrepair in the late 1800s and early 1900s, it is now a famous historical site known as **Mission Dolores**.

Bakers in the 1800s couldn't figure out why their bread was turning sour. Maybe it was all the fog in the Bay Area? But they came to love the taste. Soon everyone was calling it "sourdough" bread—a San Francisco specialty.

THE ROCK

Located in San Francisco Bay, **Alcatraz Island** was first a fort, then a military prison from 1859 until 1933, and then it became **The Rock**—the **maximum-security prison** where the worst of the worst were sent for their crimes, including Al Capone and Machine Gun Kelly. At full capacity, it housed **302 prisoners**. After closing in 1963, Alcatraz became a big tourist attraction—more than 1 million visitors come each year—and each of them is glad they are free to leave The Rock!

CROOKED, CROOKEDER, CROOKEDEST

As steep as a fast slide, the twisty downhill section of **Lombard Street** in San Francisco used to be straight. A hundred years ago, many a Model T overheated or burned out its brakes or, worse, crashed into the bushes when their drivers attempted the descent. So the city added **8 sharp turns** in 1922. Ever since, the 600-foot-long, brick-paved block of Lombard Street has been famous as **"the crookedest street in the world."**

In the summer, up to 6,000 people a day visit Lombard Street. Cars line up to go down the hill, since it's like going down a rollercoaster!

The Gold Rush had a huge impact on San Francisco. In two short years starting in 1848, the population exploded from about 800 to 25,000!

CITY RIDE

San Francisco's **44 cable cars** are art in motion. Each 8-ton car takes up to **2 years** to build, requiring a lot of fine carpentry work and fitting together of beautiful brass fixtures. You can ride a cable car by standing on a running board like BigFoot—just make sure you hold onto a pole!

GOLDEN GATE BRIDGE

Completed on **May 27, 1937**, the Golden Gate Bridge was named after the **Golden Strait**—the entrance to San Francisco Bay from the Pacific Ocean. When the sun hits the bridge, its **orange paint looks gold!** The bridge is held up by two cables that each have over 25,000 wires—the bridge is "suspended" by these cables above the water. The main span of the bridge is **4,200 feet** (1,280 m), which was the longest in the world for a suspension bridge until 1964. More than 100,000 vehicles use the bridge each day!

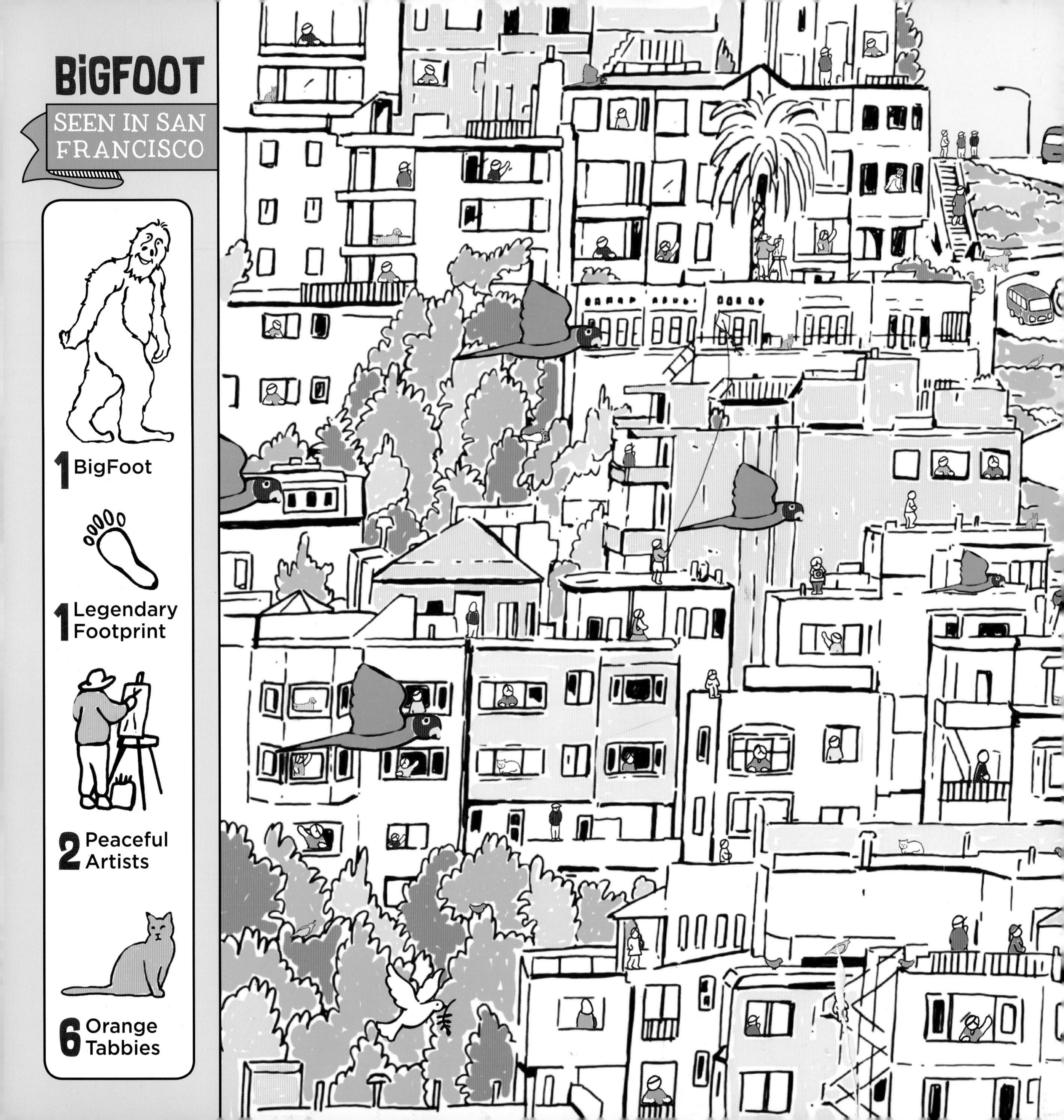
BiGFOOT
SEEN IN SAN FRANCISCO
1 BigFoot
1 Legendary Footprint
2 Peaceful Artists
6 Orange Tabbies

7 Golden Retrievers
3 Sleeping Cats
11 Wild Parrots
4 Tricky Quails
4 Red-Jacket Tourists

FORBIDDEN CITY, CHINA

CENTER OF POWER

From **1420 to 1911**, the Forbidden City was the site of the **palace** and **government buildings** of Chinese emperors, their families, and government officials. A Chinese emperor was thought to be a holy man sent from heaven, and the palace was built to show what God's home in heaven looked like. As a **holy site**, the palace and grounds were "forbidden" to regular citizens. Today, this city is open to visitors who enjoy touring the many buildings, which are filled with Chinese artifacts.

A city within a city, the famed Forbidden City is at the center of China's huge capital city, Beijing.

IMPRESSIVE ENGINEERING

It took only **15 years** to build the walls, paths, courtyards, and 1,000 buildings of the Forbidden City. That's what happened when a construction crew had over **1 million** laborers and craftsmen working full time!

While most of the Forbidden City's buildings are made out of wood, the foundations are mostly **stone**. Some of these stone blocks weigh more than **100 tons**. To get the stones from the quarry to the city, workers waited for winter. They dug wells along the route and used the water from the wells to make an **ice road**. It was much easier to slide the giant stones along the ice than along the dry ground.

CITY FORTRESS

As the place from which **Chinese emperors** ruled their country, the Forbidden City was built to withstand attacks. The city is enclosed by a **26-foot (10m)-high wall**, with a watchtower at each corner for guards to keep a lookout. A moat surrounds the outside of the city's walls.

The lion, or ***shi***, statues that fiercely guard the Forbidden City's buildings are thought to look like the lions that roamed throughout India. In ancient days, Buddhist monks traveling from India to China believed the lion represented **protection of cosmic order**, and the Chinese were quick to adopt the symbol as their own!

The little white takeout boxes from a Chinese restaurant are actually an American invention. Chicago inventor Frederick Weeks Wilcox patented his leak-proof paper box design in 1894.

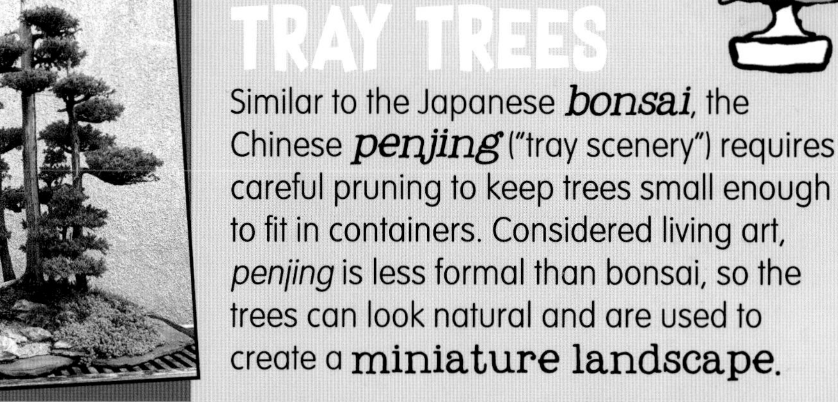

TRAY TREES

Similar to the Japanese ***bonsai***, the Chinese ***penjing*** ("tray scenery") requires careful pruning to keep trees small enough to fit in containers. Considered living art, *penjing* is less formal than bonsai, so the trees can look natural and are used to create a **miniature landscape**.

In the early 1400s, during the **Ming Dynasty**, Europeans were fascinated by the beauty of porcelain vases made in China. In 2011, one sold for over **$21 million** at auction—the world record for Ming porcelain. But most Ming vases are kept in museums so that everyone can enjoy them.

The Forbidden City opened to the public as a museum in 1925, and was declared a World Heritage Site in 1987 by the United Nations Educational, Scientific, and Cultural Organization (UNESCO).

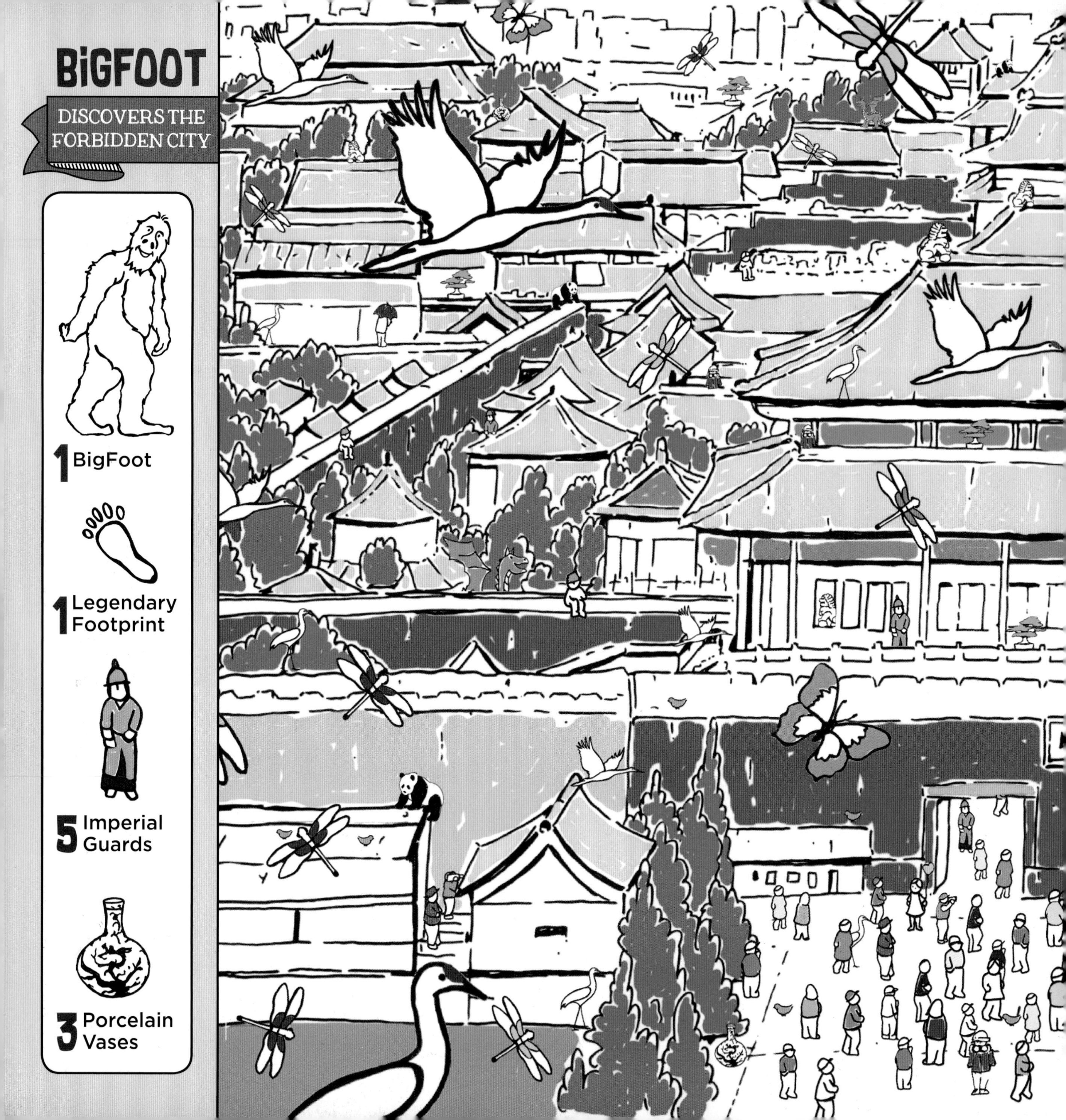
BiGFOOT
DISCOVERS THE FORBIDDEN CITY
1 BigFoot
1 Legendary Footprint
5 Imperial Guards
3 Porcelain Vases

9 Red-Crowned Cranes
8 Lion Statues
3 Friendly Green Dragons
5 Giant Pandas
7 Penjing Trees

SPLIT PERSONALITY

Istanbul, Turkey, is the only city in the world that is in both **Europe and Asia** at the same time! It straddles the two continents across the southern end of the **Bosporus Strait**—a river that's 19 miles (31 km) long running from the Black Sea to the Sea of Marmara. If Istanbul is considered a European city, then it is the biggest one in Europe—with almost **15 million** residents, it's easily bigger than Paris or London!

CITY OF MANY NAMES

Long ago Istanbul was occupied by Greeks and called **Byzantium**. When the Roman emperor Constantine (288–337 CE) relocated his capital from Rome to Byzantium in 330 CE, renaming the city **Constantinople** after himself, he established an empire that would last more than **1,000 years**. The city of Constantinople was enclosed in an enormous fortress. Well-defended, full of palaces and markets and businesses, the city housed a million people during its golden age in the **10th century**.

The Byzantine Empire ended in 1453 when Constantinople fell to invading Ottoman Turks under the command of **Sultan Muhammad II**. It was only in **1930**, after the Turks had controlled the city for almost 500 years, that Constantinople became Istanbul.

For breakfast on the go, Istanbulites love a good *simit* (freshly baked, molasses-dipped, and sesame-crusted dough).

THE HAGIA SOPHIA

The Hagia Sophia (Greek for **"divine wisdom"**) dates from 537 CE and was one of the most impressive **Greek Orthodox churches** in the world. The building that stands today is actually the **third construction**, after the first two buildings were destroyed. For the third attempt, in the 6th century Emperor Justinian I wanted the church to be bigger and better than the first two, so he had a physicist and a mathematician design it. The dome measures **102 feet** (31 m) across and took 10,000 men to build it—in just a little over **5 years!** The 4 tall, skinny minarets (spires) were added much later, in 1453, after the Ottoman Turks converted the church into a **mosque**. The building was declared a **museum** in 1935 by the first Turkish president **Mustafa Kemal Ataturk.**

Tulips, the symbol of Holland, originated in Istanbul and were sent from Istanbul to the Netherlands.

The Grand Bazaar is the biggest covered bazaar in the world, with over 3,000 shops.

BLUE MOSQUE

The most famous **landmark** in Istanbul is the Blue Mosque, completed in 1619 and named for the **20,000 blue tiles** that decorate the ceiling. The mosque is also unique because it has **6 minarets** (spires), when most mosques have 1, 2, or 4. This caused concern, because the Mecca Mosque, the holiest in the Muslim world, also had 6 minarets. So a seventh minaret was added to the Mecca Mosque to preserve its revered status. During the summer, there is a **light show** on certain nights, with facts about the mosque spoken in Turkish, English, French, and German. As a functioning mosque, it is closed to tourists for **90 minutes** at each prayer time. Around 20,000 people can worship in the mosque at the same time!

BiGFOOT
FOUND IN ISTANBUL
1 BigFoot
1 Legendary Footprint
4 Magical Oil Lamps
3 Tasty Glasses of Turkish Tea

4 Sassy Scorpions
1 Happy Flying Hummingbird
6 Yellow-Coat Street Musicians
5 Afro-Asian Parrots
9 Gleeful Turkish Dancers

ANSWER KEY

Even in the biggest cities of the world, far from his home habitat, BigFoot is an expert at staying lost. He climbs roofs, hides behind buildings, blends into crowds—it's tricky work finding him! If you were stumped the first time around, you can use this guide—the **small red dot** shows where his elusive footprint is, while the **big red dot** in each picture reveals BigFoot himself. Just as in real life, the people, animals, and objects are easier to spot than finding BigFoot, so they are not included in this answer key.

BigFoot

Legendary Footprint

Paris

New York City

Athens

London

Venice

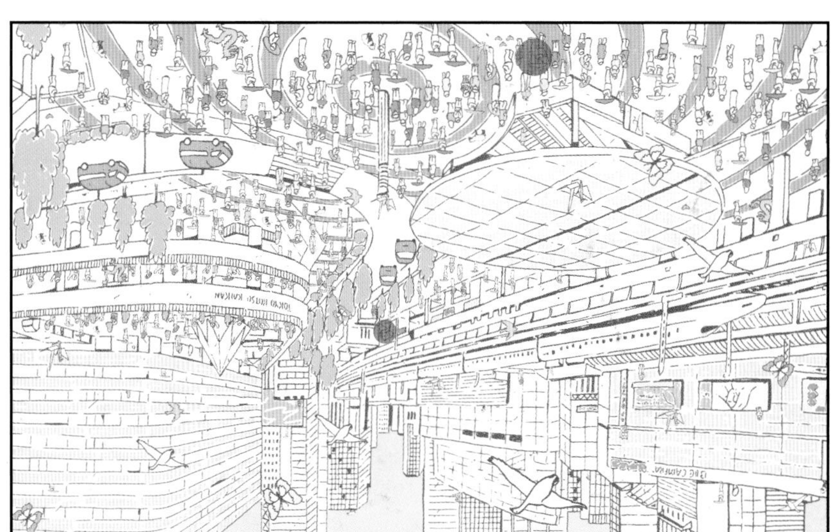
Tokyo

Toronto

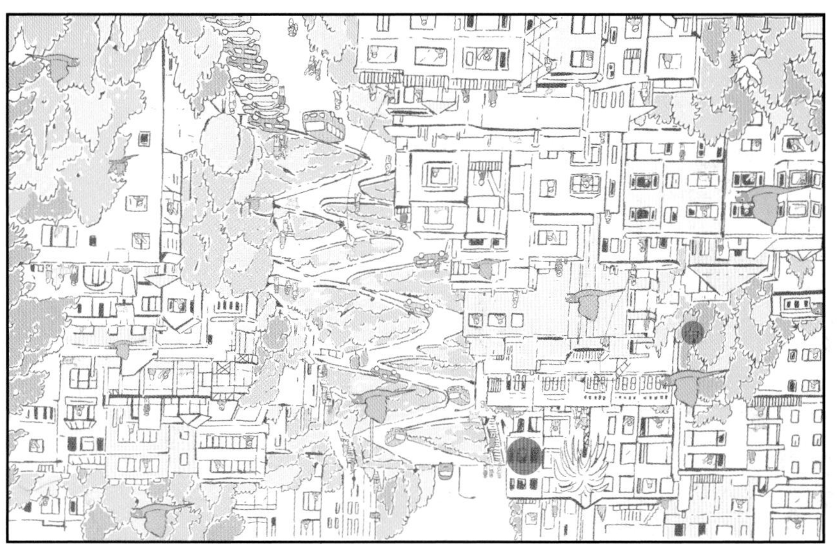
San Francisco

Forbidden City

Istanbul

ABOUT THE ARTIST

As with BigFoot, the artist and creator of this series is a bit on the elusive side. He is rarely seen in public, spending most of his days sketching in his studio located among the mighty oak trees found only in the deep, dark woods far off the beaten path.

Deeply inspired by nature, the artist spent most of his childhood tracking creatures great and small across the rocky ridgelines and wooded mountainsides, perfecting his tracking skills and keen ability to spot what many of us never see. It was once said that the artist could identify approaching hummingbirds from two counties away with one eye, while tracking a fast-moving, bouncing black bear on a pogo stick with the other eye.

Despite his many accomplishments, his most important discovery and skill is the ability to spot the deceptive BigFoot that walks among us but remains unseen by most. After spending decades learning the habits of this elusive, mythical creature, the tracker/artist has finally agreed to share his journals that capture the sightings of the infamous, larger-than-life creature that has mystified generations.

Now you have the opportunity to sharpen your search-and-find skills by finding not only BigFoot and his legendary footprint, but also the many other unusual and sometimes unexpected people, creatures, and objects that can be found at anytime . . . anywhere.

Happy Searching!

I ♥ NY